LIQUID RAW

over
125
juices, smoothies,
soups, & other raw
beverages

THE COMPLETE BOOK OF RAW FOOD

LIQUID RAW

over **125** juices, smoothies, soups, & other raw beverages

Lisa Montgomery

Hatherleigh Press is committed to preserving and protecting the natural resources of the Earth. Environmentally responsible and sustainable practices are embraced within the company's mission statement.

Hatherleigh Press is a member of the Publishers Earth Alliance, committed to preserving and protecting the natural resources of the planet while developing a sustainable business model for the book publishing industry.

This book was edited in the village of Hobart, New York. Hobart is a community that has embraced books and publishing as a component of its livelihood. There are several unique bookstores in the village. For more information, please visit www.hobartbookvillage.com.

Library of Congress Cataloging-in-Publication Data is available.
ISBN: 978-1-57826-373-8

Liquid Raw is available for bulk purchase, special promotions, and premiums. For information on reselling and special purchase opportunities, call 1-800-528-2550 and ask for the Special Sales Manager.

Cover design by DCDesign
Interior design by DCDesign

10 9 8

Printed in the United States

I want to thank everyone who made this book possible: thank you for enriching my life. My prayer is those who read this book and pick up this lifestyle will be blessed by what you have shared: many blessings.

Love,

Lisa

CONTENTS

INTRODUCTION   1

BENEFITS OF JUICING   5

LET'S GET STARTED   7

SMOOTHIES   11

MILKS AND NOGS   35

JUICES AND ELIXIRS   49

SOUPS   71

DRESSINGS, SAUCES, AND DIPS   109

PUDDINGS AND SOUFFLÉS   129

INTRODUCTION

I wrote this book as a guide for beginners as well as advanced raw foodies who want to live a healthy lifestyle. For those of you who are new to eating a raw diet, you are likely wondering how you should start incorporating healthy choices into your diet (and your family's). From my own experience, I have found that the easiest place to start is with smoothies. Whether you eat a standard American diet or are already living a healthy lifestyle, smoothies are quick and easy, and can even be used as healthy meal replacements. Juicing is another great way to start eating raw. When introducing a new smoothie or juice to your family, you may find it helpful *not* to tell them that it is good for them, as some people will automatically be turned off by healthy foods without even tasting them. Besides tasting great, juices provide high concentrations of vitamins and minerals, and work with the body to promote healing.

The recipes in *Liquid Raw* will lead you from smoothies and juicing to soups, dressings, and milks. Liquids are easier for your body to digest and easier for you to make, whether you are a novice to the raw lifestyle or are just plain busy. Too often when people start a raw diet, they go directly to making heavy raw pizzas and gourmet food, as their head keeps telling them that they are missing something because they are no longer eating a standard American diet. Somewhere along the way, we need to stop listening to our head and start listening to our body. Yes, it is wonderful to eat those gourmet delicacies once in awhile, but you will find that your body is much happier eating simple food and liquids, whether they are juices, smoothies, soups, or milks. When I look at what I consume in a day, most of my food is liquid.

So, how is this book helpful for those who are more advanced in living a healthy lifestyle? For those of you who have been eating a raw lifestyle for awhile and have been struggling with simplifying your lifestyle, *Liquid Raw* will help you to go back to the basics. The recipes in this book will inspire you and liven up your meals. It is always fun trying new recipes, even if it is simply bringing new life into old stand-bys just by adding a new twist.

Whether you are a novice or have been eating a raw diet for years, we all have our own reasons for choosing raw foods. As baby boomers, many of us thought that we somehow would be exempt from aging and getting wrinkles. Yet we were wrong, and the wrinkles came. The good news is, by living and eating healthy, I honestly feel as if I am getting younger instead of older. In fact, my general practitioner once said to me that I am the healthiest person in his practice, which sees approximately 3,500 patients. If you eat healthy, and get regular exercise and rest, chances are you will no longer need to see your doctor other than for annual check-ups. In addition to improving your overall health, a raw diet can also increase your energy levels. I personally have found that I now have so much energy that I leave the Energizer Bunny® in the dust. I always strive to be the best that I can be and to feel my best, and eating raw enables me to continue this quest.

Perhaps you are not switching to raw foods for health reasons, but because you want to look good. When you start to eat healthy, your body feels better and it shows on your face. There is a "raw glow" on the skin of those who eat healthy. I have had more people say to me, "You know why people will want to eat like you: because of your skin." I also know people who, after starting a raw diet, notice that their grey hair has turned back to their original hair color.

I know how hard it can be to transition from a standard American diet to a raw lifestyle. Rather than focusing on all of the foods that I am no longer able to eat, I prefer to introduce a new healthy drink or dish each week, which gives me something to look forward to. The biggest obstacle that I had to overcome when starting a healthy lifestyle was my own mind. When you start to introduce raw foods into your lifestyle, you can be sure that your mind will be looking instead for your old, unhealthy favorites. For me, this was a dish of ice cream with a cookie chaser. It can take a long time to win this battle, but once you start eating healthy, you will notice that you feel really great. You will also notice that, once you have been eating healthy for a while, going back to junk food can actually make you sick. This is because your body likes feeling healthy and no longer wants the junk in its system—and it lets you know it. Plus, after eating a healthy diet, you will realize that the ice cream and cookies that you once craved no longer taste as good as your mind had remembered them to be.

So, don't beat yourself up if you start to eat healthy and, once in a while, indulge in a piece of pizza. If this is going to help keep you on track the rest of the time, then so be it. Some people can successfully eat raw 100 percent of the time, while others can't (or don't want to) be that strict. It is also much more challenging to eat raw all the time if you have a spouse and kids. Trying to get them on board may be your biggest challenge, and I get that. I am single, so I was able to clear my cupboards of any unhealthy foods, although this may not be possible for everyone. So, be gentle on yourself and start with smoothies and juicing: it is the easiest and simplest way to begin living a healthy lifestyle. Plus, smoothies and juices are power-packed and sure to keep you and your family healthy.

BENEFITS OF JUICING

Juicing your fruits and vegetables can provide your body with much-needed nutrients in a tasty and convenient form. If you don't have time to make your own juices, you can turn to healthy juice bars and restaurants. More and more restaurants are also incorporating healthy choices on their menus. Even McDonalds now carries juices and smoothies. In fact, today there are companies, restaurants, and personal chefs who will make organic juices and smoothies, and deliver them to your home if you don't have the time to make them yourself. The National Cancer Institute even has begun a campaign to encourage people to eat more fruits and vegetables, recommending five servings of fruit and three servings of vegetables each day. A diet high in fruits and vegetables can help prevent (and, in some cases, cure) a wide range of ailments, and juices and smoothies are a perfect way to get all of your daily requirements. President Obama also put out a mandate for his employees to get healthier, which prompted my local government office in Philadelphia to bring me in and share with them the benefits of eating healthy and how you can implement dietary changes. As you can guess, one of the first tips that I shared was to start your day with a nutrient-packed juice or smoothie. I started by showing them how to crack open a coconut, clean out the meat and juice, and blend it in a Vitamix®. For me, the young Thai coconut is the basis of most of my smoothies.

Each recipe in this book contains fruits and vegetables that will help keep your body in top shape. Tomatoes are a common ingredient when it comes to juicing, and contain vitamins C and A, as well as several other minerals. Broccoli is another great choice as it contains anticancer compounds (called isothiocyanates) that may prevent breast cancer, while citrus, which is found in many juices, helps your body to remove carcinogens.

Here are some vegetables that contain phytochemicals, which are key to preventing some of our most deadly diseases, such as heart disease and cancer:

- bok choy
- Brussels sprouts
- cabbage
- cauliflower
- carrots
- collards
- kale
- kohlrabi
- mustard greens
- rutabaga
- turnips
- greens
- red beets
- peppers
- garlic
- onions
- leeks

LET'S GET STARTED

For any of the recipes in this book, you will need just two pieces of equipment:

Juicer – Juices are best when made using a juicer. Believe it or not, I have five different juicers (Walker, Omega, Champion, Jack LaLane™, and Tribest), but I would not expect you to go out and get all five juicers. After trying all of these juicers, my favorite has been the Tribest Green Star juicer, because it does everything. When I started my

Image courtesy of Tribest

raw diet, I was told that the Omega juicer was the best, but I found that it could only do half of what I needed. The Omega would juice the wheatgrass and greens, but was not good for hard fruits and vegetables like apples, carrots, and red beets. Plus, while it was easy to clean, I had to run the pulp through the machine several times, which was time consuming and warmed the pulp. Then I was told that the Champion juicer was the best ever, but found that it too could only handle half of what I needed (although it is great for making banana whips). Then someone told me that the Walker would be the end-all. It was huge, expensive and cumbersome. I got the Jack LaLane™ juicer at the suggestion of raw chef Dan of Quintessence, because he told me that it would create the perfect "crab-like" texture for the pulp of his "un-crab cakes," and that no other juicer would make the pulp texture look like crab cakes. So, I now use my Jack LaLane™ juicer whenever making raw crab cakes. I held off for the longest time in getting the Tribest Green Star juicer, because I heard that it had so many parts and was hard to put together. I am not very good with mechanics or technology, but I can put the Green Star together with no trouble, and I do like it best in terms of function. I can run the pulp through once, and it extracts more juice than any other juicer and is simple and easy to use. I also love that the folks at Tribest stand behind their products, and are nice and easy to work with. I have spent so much of my life taking care of others that I really love when people take care of me and stand behind their products.

High-Speed-Powered Blender – There are several high-speed-powered blenders out there, but my favorite is the Vitamix®. I have tried the Blendtec® and the Montel Williams™, and I still came away loving my Vitamix®. Last year I was in California for a book tour for my first book *Raw Inspiration, Living Dynamically with Raw Food*, and I stayed at a friend's house. She had a Blendtec® and absolutely loved it. She tried my Vitamix® and I tried her Blendtec®, but by the end of the weekend, we still loved our own blenders. Another great aspect about Vitamix® is they stand behind their equipment. If something breaks, you simply call them, and they will verify your warranty and send you a shipping label to return the blender for service, and then ship the repaired blender back to you. The Vitamix® has the speed and power to blend nuts, seeds, and ice quickly. If you attempt to make nut pates (or even

Reproduced and reprinted with the permission of Vita-Mix Corporation (www.vitamix.com)

simply juice a watermelon) in a regular blender, it just does not have the power or speed to do the job like the Vitamix® does. When traveling, the Tribest Personal blender is great, because it fits in my suit case so I can take it with me anywhere, and it has the power to make my smoothies, dressings, and pates in a compact container.

While a juicer and high-speed-powered blender are certainly investments, the good news is you will use them daily, and they will most likely last for the rest of your life. They will be worth every penny that you spend on them once you begin to enjoy your transformation to a healthy, raw diet. It is like a gosling turning into a beautiful swan or a cocoon turning into a butterfly. I want to be that swan or butterfly: don't you?

When I first started eating and drinking raw, I always followed recipes precisely, because I was accustomed to traditional cooking methods. Yet most raw chefs and teachers simply throw in ingredients without measuring. After a while, you just innately know or learn what goes well together, what you like, and how much spice that a dish needs. Raw un-cooking is more forgiving, unlike traditional cooking, where, if you do not follow the recipe precisely, the dish can be ruined. Once you become more comfortable with raw recipes, you can experiment with throwing together new dishes based on what you have available and what you are in the mood for. With raw foods, it almost always comes out really good, and if you don't quite like the taste, you can always add a pinch of this or a dollop of that. Nonetheless, for those of you who still need some assistance with your recipes, this book provides detailed recipes with step-by-step instructions. If you are advanced in raw preparation, you can use these recipes as inspiration. My mom always said that someone else's recipe always tastes better than your own, so, hopefully, this book will keep your meals exciting and maybe even spark some new ideas.

When you juice fruits and vegetables, you can add assorted supplements to kick the drink up a notch. Here are a few examples:

> Aloe vera: 100 percent pure digestive healer

> Bee pollen: promotes vitality and stamina

> Cayenne: revitalizes the respiratory system

> Vitamin C: strengthens the immune system

> Flaxseed oil: benefits the cardiovascular system

> Ginger: relieves nausea and indigestion

> Lecithin: improves brain and liver function

> Raw honey: contains healthful minerals, vitamins, carbohydrates, and enzymes (I put this in my smoothie every day). Honey is an antiseptic, antibiotic, and antibacterial, and it never spoils. It is also good for digestive disturbances.

> Maca: balances hormones

> Spirulina: boosts energy and supports cellular health

> Protein powder: helps to burn fat and build muscle

> Complete meal powder: plant-based protein that contains every nutrient necessary for optimum health (I use this every day in my smoothie)

SMOOTHIES

Smoothies are such an easy way to incorporate healthy foods into your lifestyle. People always ask me how they can begin to eat healthier, and I always tell them to start with smoothies. No matter what your eating preference, everyone loves smoothies. Kids and adults all love smoothies for various reasons. Kids love them because they are sweet, while parents and many adults love them because they are healthy, tasty, and easy to make. Seniors also love smoothies because they slide down easily without requiring any chewing, which often becomes a challenge for seniors. Smoothies are also easy to digest. When my mom was sick, I would often go to my parent's house and make several pitchers full of smoothies for her to drink throughout the week. It is also handy to have a pitcher of smoothies made for your kids to drink when they come home from school. This is a delicious, yet healthy, alternative to a bag of potato chips or cookies.

Smoothies are also great meal replacements. I drink a smoothie for breakfast every day after I finish juicing my wheatgrass. They are so convenient because, even when you are half asleep in the morning, all that you need to do is throw everything in the high-speed blender, blend, and drink – it's that simple. In fact, when I know that I have to get up extra early (which I hate doing), I will make my smoothie the night before, and store it in a glass jar so I can drink it for breakfast when I am driving the next morning. A lot of people also drink green smoothies as meal replacements for breakfast, lunch, or dinner.

Strawberry-Pear-Cucumber Smoothie

Alorah Arliotis (www.thewiserwoman.co.uk), Glastonbury, England

Prep: 10 minutes

1 peeled cucumber
3 pears, cut up
2 kiwis, peeled
4 strawberries
½ cup fresh mint, trimmed
2 cups water
1 teaspoon agave

Combine all ingredients in a high-speed blender and blend.

Tropical Smoothie

Alorah Arliotis (www.thewiserwoman.co.uk), Glastonbury, England

Prep: 7 minutes

4 bananas
2 pears
Handful spinach
1 kiwi, peeled and sliced
3 dates, pitted and soaked
8 ounces coconut water
1 frozen wheatgrass shot
Water

Combine ingredients in a high-speed blender and enjoy.

WHEATGRASS

If you don't want to grow your own wheatgrass, you can buy it from local growers. You can buy it already cut and bagged or on a flat so you can cut it yourself. If you juice nothing else, I strongly urge you to start your day by juicing wheatgrass. It is full of vitamins and minerals, which makes it cleansing, healing, and detoxifying. Wheatgrass is a stand-alone juice. I start almost every day by juicing several ounces. I do not combine wheatgrass with anything else. It is also best to drink on an empty stomach. Remember: you should not drink wheatgrass quickly. Instead, sip and swish a mouthful at a time.

Not only does wheatgrass keep me strong and healthy on a daily basis, but I have also encountered an amazing experience with wheatgrass. A few years ago, I stopped juicing wheatgrass due to some financial challenges. After I went a month or so without juicing wheatgrass, I noticed that a quarter-sized lump had appeared on my breast. I kept hoping it would go away, but it didn't. So, I made an appointment with my doctor to have it removed. Then I remembered my DVD from Dr. Lorraine Day, an emergency room surgeon who had a very large lump on her breast who decided to change her diet and lifestyle instead of using surgery and chemotherapy. So, I cancelled the doctor appointment and went back to juicing the wheatgrass. In a very short period of time, the lump disappeared and has never returned. I will never again go without juicing wheatgrass routinely, no matter what my economic status. Some folks even rub wheatgrass juice on their face, while others do wheatgrass implants when having a colonic or enema.

Green Smoothie

Victoria Boutenko, The Raw Family, author of many books such as Green for Life *and* The 12 Steps to Raw Food

Victoria invented the Green Smoothie as her health had plateaued, and she was looking for another way to get greens into her system—and yes, believe it or not, there are only so many green salads that a person can eat in a day. Victoria has written several books on the Green Smoothies, which contain many recipes and nutritional findings. In fact, Harvard now recognizes the health benefits of Green Smoothies.

Spinach
1 big stalk kale
2 bananas
1 apple
1 pear
5 dates, pitted
Water and ice as needed

Blend ingredients together in a high-speed blender and serve.

Green Radiance Beauty Smoothie

Janice Innella, The Beauty Chef

Janice has such a gift when she creates food. Her creations have wonderful layers and flavors, and the presentation is always beautiful. Her creations are as beautiful as she is—on the outside and in.

4 pieces romaine
1 bunch each parsley, dill, and mint
2 tablespoons sprouted sunflower seeds or whatever is available
½ avocado
1 organic apple or pear
1 tablespoon raw cacao powder
Pinch Celtic sea salt
Pinch cayenne pepper
1 cup filtered water
1 tablespoon raw honey or agave to taste

Blend in high-speed blender until creamy and smooth. Garnish with celery or strawberry.

Tropical Snow Smoothie

Lisa Montgomery

1 mango or papaya
1 1-inch slice fresh pineapple
1 tray ice cubes
3 bananas
1 young Thai coconut (meat and juice)
Handful cacao nibs
1 tablespoon raw honey

Combine all of the ingredients in a high-speed blender.

You may be wondering why I called this smoothie Tropical Snow Smoothie. It was because when I came up with this recipe for breakfast, it was snowing.

Strawberry Choco-Nanna Smoothie

Lisa Montgomery

3 fresh bananas
1 tray ice cubes
1 cup strawberries
1–2 heaping tablespoons raw cacao or carob powder
1 teaspoon raw honey or agave syrup
2 cups almond milk

In a high-powered blender, blend all ingredients and blend until creamy. Pour into drinking glasses and enjoy.

Lisa's Breakfast Smoothie

Lisa Montgomery

3 bananas
2 cups almond milk
4–8 ounces fresh fruit
12 ice cubes
1 tablespoon raw cacao nibs
1 tablespoon raw honey
1 tablespoon Vega® Complete Whole Food Health Optimizer
    (I use Vanilla Chai)

Combine all ingredients in a Vitamix® and blend until smooth.

Lisa's Green Smoothie

Lisa Montgomery

3 bananas
2 pears
1-inch-thick slice fresh pineapple
1 tablespoon raw honey
3–4 leaves kale or assorted greens
1 young Thai coconut (meat and water)

Add all ingredients to a high-speed blender and blend until smooth.
Pour into a glass and drink.

Frog (Fig-Raspberry-Orange-Ginger) Smoothie

Lisa Montgomery

3 figs, pitted
1½ cups raspberries
2 oranges, peeled and seeded
¼-inch piece ginger
3 bananas
1 young Thai coconut
1 tray ice cubes

Combine all of the ingredients together in a high-speed blender and enjoy.

Kimberton's Ginger-Mint Green Smoothie

Dave Biddison, Café Manager
Kimberton Whole Foods, Kimberton, PA

Kimberton Whole Foods has four locations of health markets in southeastern Pennsylvania. Besides the markets, they also have a healthy restaurant. Kimberton Whole Foods is one of my "home away from home" places. They have such warmth, kind of like Cheers, *where everyone knows your name. I hope that you have a place like this near you. If you don't, you may want to start one in your neighborhood.*

Yield: 32 ounces or 2 16-ounce cups

2 cups fresh green spinach, washed and packed
2 whole apples, washed and chopped coarsely (seeds and all)
1 teaspoon pureed ginger
10 leaves fresh mint
½ lemon, juiced
2 cups filtered water

Combine the ingredients together in a high-speed blender.

Coconut Curry

Raw Chef Dan, Quintessence, New York, NY, and Crucina,
Madrid, Spain

1 cup water
1 cup coconut water from young Thai coconut
½ cup coconut meat from young Thai coconut, chopped
3 tablespoon coconut flakes
1½ tablespoons minced ginger
1½ tablespoons raw soy sauce
½ tablespoon chili powder
½ teaspoon curry powder
½ red bell pepper
½ teaspoon coconut butter
1 small clove garlic

Blend all of the ingredients together in a high-speed blender. Chill and serve.

Apple Cinnamon Whip

Raw Chef Dan, Quintessence, New York, NY, and Crucina, Madrid, Spain

Whip
12 ounces apple juice
1 teaspoon flax oil
¼ teaspoon cinnamon

Macadamia Vanilla Icing
1 cup macadamia nuts
½ cup water
¼ cup raw agave or honey
2 tablespoons vanilla
½ teaspoon sea salt

Whip
Combine in a high-speed blender and blend. Serve with a cinnamon stick and top with a spoonful of Macadamia Vanilla Icing (see below).

Macadamia Vanilla Icing
Blend together in a high-speed blender until smooth. Refrigerate for 2 hours before serving.

Banana Lasse

Raw Chef Dan, Quintessence, New York, NY, and Crucina, Madrid, Spain

Yogurt Blend
1 young Thai coconut (½ cup meat, chopped)
¼ cup water
1½ teaspoon lemon juice
1 teaspoon agave
¼ teaspoon sea salt
3 drops Live Live™ propolis

Lasse
1 cup ice, crushed
½ ripe banana
¼ teaspoon cardamom

Combine both together and enjoy.

Date-Coco Shake

The Date People (www.datepeople.net)
The Date People are growers of dates in California.

1 young Thai coconut
14 dates, pitted
Ice

Drain coconut water into a blender. Split open the coconut and spoon out meat the inside into the blender. Add dates and ice, and give it a whirl. For variety, add strawberries, vanilla bean, or banana.

Pumpkin Smoothie

Sheryll Chavarria, Raw Can Roll Café and Pure Body Spa,
Douglassville, PA (www.rawcanrollcafe.com)

8 ounces almond milk
1 cup pumpkin, chopped
½ banana, frozen
1 teaspoon pumpkin spice (or to taste)

Combine all of the ingredients together in a high-speed blender. If the smoothie is too watery, blend in ice cubes.

Green smoothies are so nutritious (about sixty percent fruit with about forty percent green vegetables). They taste like fruit, but have all the nutrition found in dark leafy greens. When you are first starting, you may want to use fewer greens and let your taste buds develop a taste for them (especially when getting children to drink green smoothies). You can also use blueberries to disguise the color. When blended well, all of the valuable nutrients become easy for the body to digest. As opposed to juices, green smoothies are a complete food because they still have fiber.

Strawberry-Goji Berry Smoothie

Joel Odhner, Catalyst Cleanse, Rawlife Line, Philadelphia, PA

1 fresh young Thai coconut (meat and water)
1 cup strawberries, chopped into small pieces
1 tablespoon agave
¼ cup goji berries, soaked

Combine the above ingredients together in a high-speed blender. Chill and serve.

Remember to buy organic strawberries, because conventional strawberries are known for containing high levels of pesticides.

Option: this smoothie also tastes great by adding 2–3 oranges (meat only).

Pomegranate Smoothie

Tonya Zavasta, author of many books such as Your Right to Be Beautiful: The Miracle of Raw Foods *(www.beautifulonraw.com)*

Serves 2

2 cups pomegranate juice (use Tribest's Citrastar juicer to juice pomegranates)
1 cup frozen fruit, such as blueberries, mango, or mixed berries
2 ripe bananas
1 leaf romaine lettuce

Combine all of the above together in a high-speed blender.

Be careful when purchasing frozen fruit as it may contain added refined sugar or preservatives, which will defeat the purpose of trying to eat and live a healthy lifestyle. The best way to make sure that there are no preservatives or sugar in your frozen fruit is to freeze it yourself. When my fruit comes in, I use it as well as freeze it. When organic fruit is on sale at my local market, I will also buy several cases and freeze them so I can pull them out when I need them.

Chock-LICK-ity Super Smoothie

Potlucker Denise DiJoseph (www.miaura.com)

This drink satisfies my occasional chocolate shake craving and gives me lots of energy to last through a long day.

Prep: 15 minutes

2 scoops Amazing Grass® Green SuperFood® Chocolate Drink
    Powder
2 tablespoons Vitamineral™ Green Powder
2 tablespoons flaxseed, ground
1 tablespoon maca powder
3 tablespoons hempseed, ground
3 tablespoons chia gel
4 tablespoons sesame seeds
2 tablespoons coconut crème
4 tablespoons raw cacao powder
Pinch Himalayan or red salt
Meat of 1 young Thai coconut (reserve the water)
3 frozen bananas
2–3 medjool dates, pitted
3 tablespoons goji berries
1 tray ice cubes
Agave to taste (optional)

Add all the ingredients in the order listed into a high-powered blender. Add the coconut water as needed to achieve the desired consistency of a thick chocolate milk shake.

Tutti Fruitti

Sheryll Chavarria, Raw Can Roll Café and Pure Body Spa, Douglassville, PA (www.rawcanrollcafe.com)

Sheryll combines an all-natural, organic food café and smoothie bar with an all-natural, organic, and safe body care center. You can take care of the outside as well as the in.

10 ounces fresh-pressed apple juice
1 cup frozen berries
½ cup frozen banana
½ cup ice (optional)
Agave to taste

Place ingredients in a high-speed blender. Blend well.

Down on the Bayou

Sheryll Chavarria, Raw Can Roll Café and Pure Body Spa, Douglassville, PA (www.rawcanrollcafe.com)

10 ounces coconut milk (can add coconut meat, as well)
1½ cups frozen pineapple
¼ banana (for texture)
½ cup ice (optional)
Agave to taste

Combine ingredients together in a high-speed blender. Blend well and enjoy.

Apple-Banana-Pear Smoothie

Lisa Montgomery

2 pears, seeded and cored

3 bananas

1 apple, seeded and cored

1 tablespoon raw honey

Handful raw cacao nibs

1 tablespoon Vanilla Chai Complete Whole Food Health
        Optimizer by Sequel Naturals, Ltd.

1 tray ice cubes

1 raw egg (optional)

Combine the above ingredients together in a high-speed blender. Blend well and enjoy.

Every Monday and Thursday, I put an egg in my smoothie since raw eggs are a great source of B12. I have my own chickens so I can walk out each morning and get fresh eggs. I would only recommend this if you know that your body needs it and you know where the eggs are coming from. I know my "girls" (chickens) eat the same healthy food that I do, such as juice pulp, wheatgrass pulp, and watermelon rinds. Sometimes, I will also give them bread and other leftovers that I bring home from a restaurant (some people have doggy bags; I have chicken bags).

Start Me Up Energy Rx Smoothie (Acai, Apple, Mango, Strawberry, Pineapple)

Susan Barrett, Roby Nagy, Strawberry Fields Juice and Smoothie Bar, Phoenixville, PA

16 ounces Rx Smoothie (see note below)

8 ounces fresh apple juice

1 Sambazon Acai Packet

2 ounces mango

2 ounces strawberry

2 ounces pineapple

Blend together on speed number 5 in a Vitamix® for 20 seconds. Pour into a 16-ounce cup and enjoy.

An Rx Smoothie begins with a standard smoothie and adds a supplement that may be used for a specific purpose (in this case, it is acai with gaurana, which gives you energy).

Green Goodness Smoothie (Organic Kale, Banana, Cantaloupe, Pineapple)

Susan Barrett, Roby Nagy, Strawberry Fields Juice and Smoothie Bar, Phoenixville, PA

12 ounce smoothie (see note below)
3 large leaves kale
1 cup banana
½ cup cantaloupe
½ cup pineapple
1 cup ice

For a complete meal, add 1 ounce of whey or hemp protein. For added nutrition, add 1 scoop of Green Vibrance Powder. Blend together in a Vitamix® on speed number 3 for 20 seconds. Pour into a 12-ounce cup.

A smoothie includes all parts of the fruit or veggie, which should be washed and/or peeled before blending.

Carrot-Banana-Ginger Smoothie

*Dave Biddison, Café Manager, Kimberton Whole Foods Café,
Kimberton Whole Foods, Kimberton, PA*

Yield: 32 ounces or 2 16-ounce cups

1½ cups filtered water
2 whole apples, washed and chopped coarsely (seeds and all)
1 banana
1 cup fresh carrots (grated carrots are easier to measure)
½ cup orange juice
½ lemon, juiced
1 teaspoon ginger, pureed

Blend on number 3 and then number 6 speeds in a Vitamix®
blender.

Berry Green Smoothie

*David Biddison, Café Manager, Kimberton Whole Foods Café,
Kimberton Whole Foods, Kimberton, PA*

Yield: 32 ounces or 2 16-ounce cups.

2 cups filtered water
2 cups frozen raspberries
2 whole apples, washed and chopped coarsely (seeds and all)
1½ cups fresh spinach, washed and packed
1 heaping teaspoon minced ginger

Blend on number 3 and then number 6 speeds using your Vitamix®
blender.

Raspberry-Banana Yogurt Smoothie

David Biddision, Café Manager, Kimberton Whole Foods Café,
Kimberton Whole Foods, Kimberton, PA

Yield: 32 ounces or 2 16-ounce cups

2 cups frozen raspberries
1½ bananas
1 cup Seven Stars Plain Yogurt (please note that this is not raw)
1 cup filtered water
1 tablespoon maple syrup

Blend on number 3 and then number 6 speeds on your Vitamix®
blender.

Cayenne-Honey-Kale Smoothie

David Biddison, Café Manager, Kimberton Whole Foods Café,
Kimberton Whole Foods, Kimberton, PA

Yield: 32 ounces or 2 16-ounce cups

2 cups filtered water
2 whole apples, washed and chopped coarsely (seeds and all)
2 cups fresh kale, washed and packed
1 lemon, juiced
2 tablespoons raw honey
1 teaspoon ginger, pureed
¼ teaspoon ground cayenne

Blend on number 3 and then number 6 speeds in a Vitamix®
blender.

Ginger-Mint Green Smoothie

Dave Biddison, Café Manager, Kimberton Whole Foods Café,
Kimberton Whole Foods, Kimberton, PA

Yield: 32 ounces or 2 16-ounce cups

2 cups filtered water
2 whole apples, washed and chopped coarsely (seeds and all)
2 cups fresh spinach, washed and packed
½ lemon, juiced
1 teaspoon ginger, pureed
10 leaves fresh mint (approximately)

Blend on number 3 speed in a Vitamix® blender.

Cranberry Smoothie

Dave Biddision, Café Manager, Kimberton Whole Foods Café,
Kimberton Whole Foods, Kimberton, PA

Yield: 32 ounces or 2 16-ounce cups

1½ cups filtered water
1 cup fresh-organic cranberries, well-washed (or frozen will do)
1 whole apple, washed and chopped coarsely (seeds and all)
½ orange, well-washed (rind, seeds, and all)
½ cup fresh orange juice
½ cup fresh carrot (grated carrots are easier to measure)
1 teaspoon ground cinnamon

Blend on number 3 speed in a Vitamix® blender.

MILKS AND NOGS

Milks and nogs not only taste good (and, of course, are good for you), but for me, they are also emotionally comforting drinks. Just picture sipping almond milk or nog out of a hand-made pottery cup while sitting by the fire place: it doesn't get any better than that. Almond milk can be used on its own or incorporated into another recipe. For example, I use almond milk as one of the foundational ingredients to my breakfast smoothies on the days that I don't use a young Thai coconut. Remember that, when you strain your milks and nogs, you can save the pulp and turn it into crackers, croutons, or scones or feed it to your pets or outdoor wildlife.

Almond Milk

Tribest, Home of the Green Star Juicer and Sedona Dehydrator
This recipe is from the folks at Tribest and is designed to be made in
their Soyabella.

Prep: 15 minutes
Soak: almonds, 6–8 hours

1 cup almonds, soaked and drained
2 cups water
1 tablespoon maple syrup
1 teaspoon vanilla

Blend the above ingredients together until smooth and creamy.
Strain liquid in a milk bag or fine strainer using a large bowl. Store
in a sealed glass jar. Serve cold in glass.

Maple-Almond Milk

Make in Tribest Soyabella milk maker

Prep: 25 minutes
Soak: almonds, 4–6 hours

1 cup almonds, soaked/rinsed (2.5 ounces)
0.8 liter or approximately 3 cups (27 fluid ounces) filtered water
     (fill to the lower line in Soyabella chamber)
2–5 tablespoons maple syrup (grade B is best)
1 teaspoon alcohol-free vanilla
1–2 pinches sea salt

Fill the chamber with 0.8 liter (approximately 3 cups or 27 fluid ounces) of filtered water (to the lower line).

Fill the milk screen with soaked almonds and attach to the heat unit, turning counter-clockwise. Make sure it is secure.

Follow instructions for making raw nut milk.

Pour the unflavored almond milk in a glass container. Combine almond milk with maple syrup, vanilla, and sea salt.

Chill before serving.

Chocolate-Cashew Milk

Raw Chef Dan, Quintessence, New York, NY, and Crucina,
Madrid, Spain

Prep: 15 minutes

3½ cups water
½ cup cashews
¼ cup cacao powder or nibs
1 tablespoon coconut butter
2 tablespoon agave
1 teaspoon vanilla
½ teaspoon sea salt

Blend all the ingredients together in a high-speed blender. Chill and serve.

For a smoother drink, you can strain the milk through a nut bag, which removes the nut pulp. You can also save the nut pulp and turn it into crackers, croutons, scones, or nut flours. Also, try serving it to your pets or wildlife in your backyard.

Elaina's Nut Nog

Elaina Love, author of Pure Joy Kitchen *(www.purejoyplanet.com)*

Several years ago, I was on the hunt for a raw egg nog recipe. I kept trying to find the best egg nog recipe, and many of my raw chef friends came to my rescue. Try this recipe and the ones on the following pages to see which is your favorite.

Prep: 20 minutes
Soak: almonds, 8–24 hours

1 cup almonds, soaked

¼ cup pine nuts

2½ cups filtered water

2–3 frozen bananas, cut into chunks

4–5 medium dates, pitted (soak if firm and use the soaking
      water in place of water)

½ teaspoon nutmeg

½ teaspoon ground cloves

1 teaspoon vanilla extract

2 teaspoons flax oil

Pinch Celtic sea salt

Blend the nuts and water, and strain the pulp out using a nut milk bag.

    Combine the milk mixture with the remaining ingredients in a high-speed blender and blend until smooth.

Nut Nog

Joel Odhner, Catalyst Cleanse, Rawlife Line, Philadelphia, PA

Prep: 15 minutes

2 cups almond milk
4 dates, pitted
½ banana (frozen works best)
½ teaspoon vanilla
Pinch cardamom
Nutmeg to taste

Combine the above ingredients together in a high-speed blender. Store in a glass jar. Chill and serve.

Egg Nog

Janice Innella, The Beauty Chef

Prep: 20 minutes

3 cups almond milk or Brazil nut milk (you make Brazil nut
      milk the same way that you make almond milk)

2 cups cashews

2 young coconuts (meat only)

2 vanilla beans

1 teaspoon nutmeg

Pinch cloves

½ teaspoon garam masala

3 teaspoons stevia or ½ cup agave or 6 tablespoons raw honey

1 teaspoon cinnamon (or to taste)

Blend together well in a high-speed blender until creamy. Chill for
a few hours. Serve with a sprinkle of nutmeg on top for garnish.

Un-Egg Nog

Lisa Montgomery

Prep: 15 minutes

2 cups almond milk
3 fresh bananas
¼ teaspoon Sun Organics alcohol-free vanilla extract
¼ teaspoon cinnamon
Pinch sea salt
2–3 dates pitted
¼ teaspoon nutmeg, grated (or to taste)

Place all the ingredients in a high-speed blender and blend until smooth. Add additional dates if you wish the nog to be sweeter. Serve immediately with a dash of grated nutmeg on top.

Live Almond Nog for Holiday Comfort

Victoria Boutenko, The Raw Family, author of many books such as
Green for Life *and* The 12 Steps to Raw Food

*Victoria Boutenko is a world-renowned author and speaker on raw
foods. Her creation of the Green Smoothie has taken raw foods to
another dimension. Everyone now has their own green smoothie thanks
to Victoria, who created the original Green Smoothie.*

Serves 4
Prep: 15 minutes
Soak: almonds, overnight

1 cup raw almonds, soaked overnight
2 cups water
4–5 dates, pitted
1 teaspoon nutmeg, ground
¼ teaspoon sea salt (optional)

Thoroughly blend ingredients together in a high-speed blender
until smooth. Strain mixture through a nut milk bag. Pour into a
jar and chill.

Chocolate-Cherry Shake

Mathew Kenney, Mathew Kenney's Academy and author of Everyday Raw *and* Entertaining in the Raw

Mathew is the co-founder of the 105 Degrees School in Oklahoma. Mathew has written numerous books, and has been involved with countless restaurants and projects around the globe. I was honored to have him speak at several raw potlucks and to have taken several of his raw cooking classes. He is considered a genius in the kitchen. What is truly amazing is he still has a kind heart and always takes the time to answer your questions—and no question is ever silly in his eyes. This is one of my absolute favorite drinks; I love it.

Serves 4
Prep: 15 minutes

2 cups frozen cherries
2 cups frozen bananas (or 2 fresh bananas)
¼ cup cacao nibs
1 cup coconut water
2 tablespoons agave
1 teaspoon alcohol-free vanilla extract
Pinch sea salt

Blend all of the ingredients together in a high-speed blender on high for 30–40 seconds.

Thai Green Smoothie with Spirulina and Coconut

Mathew Kenney, Mathew Kenney's Academy and author of Everyday Raw *and* Entertaining in the Raw

Serves 4
Prep: 15 minutes

4 cups frozen pineapple chunks
1 frozen banana
1 cup young Thai coconut (meat only)
2 cups spinach, packed
2 tablespoons agave
2 tablespoons coconut butter
2 cups coconut water
1 teaspoon spirulina
1 Thai green chili (seeds removed)
1 teaspoon vanilla extract
Pinch sea salt

Blend all of the above ingredients together in a high-speed blender on high for 30–40 seconds.

Strawberry-Banana Shake

Mathew Kenney, Mathew Kenney's Academy and author of Everyday Raw *and* Entertaining in the Raw

Serves 4
Prep: 10 minutes

5 cups frozen strawberries
2 cups frozen bananas
1½ cups almond milk

Blend all of the ingredients together in a high-speed blender on high for 30–40 seconds.

Vanilla Bean Shake

Mathew Kenney, Mathew Kenney's Academy and author of Everyday Raw *and* Entertaining in the Raw

Serves 4
Prep: 15 minutes

4 cups frozen bananas, chopped (about 4 bananas)
4 teaspoon alcohol-free vanilla extract
½ vanilla bean, scraped
2 cups almond milk
Pinch sea salt

Blend all of the ingredients together in a high-speed blender on high for about 30–40 seconds.

Almond Milk

Mathew Kenney, Mathew Kenney's Academy and author of Everyday Raw *and* Entertaining in the Raw

Prep: 15 minutes
Soak: almonds, 12 hours

1 cup raw almonds (soaked for 12 hours)
4 cups water
2 tablespoons extra virgin coconut oil
2 tablespoons agave
1 teaspoon vanilla extract
Pinch sea salt

Blend ingredients together in a high-speed blender for at least 1 minute. Strain through a chinois, nut milk bag, or cheesecloth. Use a ladle to push as much liquid through as possible. Serve or store in a refrigerator for up to 3 days.

You can adjust the amount of servings for this recipe by using a 4-to-1 ratio (1 cup almonds to 4 cups water).

Brazil Nut Milk

Mathew Kenney, Mathew Kenney's Academy and author of Everyday Raw *and* Entertaining in the Raw

Yield: 1 quart
Prep: 20 minutes
Soak: Brazil nuts, 4–6 hours

1 cup Brazil nuts (soaked for 4–6 hours)
4 cups water
2 tablespoons extra virgin coconut oil
¼ cup agave
1 teaspoon alcohol-free vanilla extract
Pinch sea salt

Blend all of the ingredients together in a high-speed blender for at least 1 minute. Strain through a chinois, nut milk bag, or cheese-cloth. Use a ladle to push as much liquid through as possible. Serve or store in a refrigerator for up to 3 days.

Here are some handy tips for juicing:

When juicing, place the fine screen over the twin gears. Then attach the pulp discharge casing with the outlet, adjusting the knob in place, and loosen the knob as you juice to allow the pulp to come out (when I juice wheatgrass, I do not use the knob, at all). Place the pitcher under the juice outlet to catch the juice, and keep a bowl or bag under the pulp discharge outlet to catch the pulp. Remember to save your pulp, as you can use it in crackers and burgers or even feed it to your pets. My dogs and chickens eat my juice pulp (that is if I don't use it myself).

Scarlet Beauty Juice

Tonya Zavasta, author of Beautiful on Raw: unCooked Creations *(www.beautifulonraw.com)*

Prep: 10 minutes

5 medium tomatoes
2 medium carrots
1 medium beet root

Juice all the ingredients and drink immediately.

Ruby Rejuvenating Juice

*Tonya Zavasta, author of Beautiful on Raw: unCooked Creations
(www.beautifulonraw.com)*

Prep: 10 minutes

4 stalks celery
3 medium carrots
1 medium beet root
1 medium apple
½ lemon (with the skin)

Juice all the ingredients and drink immediately.

Cleanse Fast Drink

Lisa Montgomery

*When I have done cleanse fasts, I would juice Granny Smith apples
and drink eight ounces every one-and-a-half hours. I have done fasts
anywhere from one day to (believe it or not) nine days.*

Prep: 10 minutes

4 Granny Smith apples
4 ounces water

Juice apples and combine with water. Store the juice in glass jars
with lids, and shake it up when ready to drink to combine the apple
and water.

Liver Cleanse Drink

Lisa Montgomery

Prep: 10 minutes

Red beets
Kale
Water (optional)

Juice equal parts kale and red beets, combine, and drink.

Arugula Pear Juice

Raw Chef Dan, Quintessence, New York, NY, and Crucina, Madrid, Spain

1 handful fresh arugula
1 small cucumber
2 stalks celery
1 pear
½ medium red or yellow bell pepper
½ lemon, squeezed

Juice all the ingredients in a juicer, and then serve.

Beauty Elixir Cocktail: Cinnamon Hot Toddy

Janice Innella, The Beauty Chef

6 cups water

2 cups coconut water or almond milk

1 teaspoon cardamom

1 teaspoon garam masala

1 teaspoon ginger

½ teaspoon black pepper

1 teaspoon nutmeg

1 teaspoon clove

2 vanilla beans or 1 tablespoon vanilla extract

1 tablespoon cinnamon

Heat water to a boil. Bring down to a simmer, add all the spices, and simmer for 15 minutes. Serve with a cinnamon stick and a dollop of coconut butter.

Beauty Elixir: Pomegranate-tini

Janice Innella, The Beauty Chef

2 beets

1 pomegranate

1 teaspoon ginger powder

2 cups coconut water

Combine the above in a high-speed blender. Pour the elixir through a nut milk bag to strain out the pulp. Serve chilled in a martini glass with a mint or pomegranate seed garnish.

Better than V8® Juice

Rhonda Malkmus, Hallelujah Acres, Shelby, NC

Prep: 15 minutes

Carrots (approximately ½ pound or enough to make 4 ounces
    of juice)
Handful cherry tomatoes
1 small beet
2 small ribs
½ medium cucumber, peeled
10 baby spinach leaves
2 lettuce leaves
2 stems parsley
⅛-inch-thick slice ginger

Prepare ingredients and run through a juicing machine. Strain
juice and enjoy.

Invigorating Emerald Juice

Tonya Zavasta, author of Beautiful on Raw: unCooked Creations
(www.beautifulonraw.com)

Prep: 10 minutes

1 stem broccoli
3 stalks celery
3 cucumbers
2 medium Granny Smith apples

Juice all the ingredients and drink immediately.

Ponceau Pomegranate Punch

Tonya Zavasta, author of Beautiful on Raw: unCooked Creations
(www.beautifulonraw.com)

Prep: 15 minutes

1 pomegranate
1 medium orange, juiced
½ inch ginger root
1 tablespoon raw honey

Squeeze a pomegranate in your hands until the seeds inside release their juice. Place the pomegranate in a small plastic bag while squeezing to avoid getting splashed if the skin of the pomegranate breaks open. When the pomegranate feels very soft, make a small cut and squeeze the juice into a container. Put through a strainer to remove the seeds or their pieces. Make orange and ginger root juice in a juicing machine. Combine juices and add raw honey. Chill before serving.

Ginger Spritzer

Janice Innella, The Beauty Chef

1 cup fresh ginger, peeled and chopped small
2 limes
6 cups pure water or Pellegrino® water
2 tablespoons raw honey or agave

Combine the ingredients together in a high-speed blender. Run through a strainer and serve chilled with a twist of lime.

Peppermint Water

Lisa Montgomery

Pitcher purified water, chilled
Ice
Drop or 2 mint extract (to taste)
Stevia, agave, or raw honey to taste

Combine the ingredients together and you will have the most refreshing summer drink.

Holiday Rum Piña Colada

Frederic Patenaude's New Year Menu (www.fredericpatenaude.com)

¼ large pineapple or ½ small pineapple, chilled, peeled, and
    coarsely chopped
1 young Thai coconut (water and meat), chilled
½ teaspoon rum extract (optional)
Agave syrup to sweeten (optional)
Ice cubes as desired

Blend all of the ingredients together in a high-speed blender until smooth, adding ice cubes to achieve desired consistency. Sweeten if desired.

Piña Colada

Raw Chef Dan, Quintessence, New York, NY, and Crucina,
Madrid, Spain

1 cup ice, crushed
½ cup pineapple, chopped
½ cup coconut water
3 tablespoons coconut flakes (dried coconut)
1 teaspoon raw agave
1 teaspoon lemon juice

Combine all of the ingredients together in a high-speed blender.

Strawberry-Mango Coulis

Lisa Montgomery

Prep: 15 minutes

3 cups strawberries, hulled
1 cup mango, cubed
1 cup dates,pitted and packed
1 tablespoon lemon juice
½ tablespoon lime juice
Water (as needed)

Combine ingredients in a high speed-blender and use water as needed to blend well. Refrigerate in a glass jar with lid.

Watermelon-Strawberry Thirst Quencher

Lisa Montgomery

Prep: 15 minutes

3 cups watermelon
1 cup strawberries
1 lime, juiced
2 dates, pitted
1 tray ice cubes

Combine the above ingredients in a Vitamix® blender.

Raspberry Lemonade

Mathew Kenney, Mathew Kenney's Academy and author of Everyday Raw *and* Entertaining in the Raw, *as taught by Ladan Raissi, 105 Degrees at Natural Gourmet Institute for Health and Culinary Arts, New York, NY*

Serves 2

3 cups water
1 cup lemon juice
½ cup agave
8–10 frozen raspberries

Mix water, lemon juice, and agave together. Chill well and serve in tall glasses. Add 4–5 frozen raspberries to each before serving.

Lemon juice is helpful in breaking up fatty deposits.

Spicy C with Goji Berries

Mathew Kenney, Mathew Kenney's Academy and author of Everyday Raw *and* Entertaining in the Raw, *as taught by Ladan Raissi, 105 Degrees at Natural Gourmet Institute for Health and Culinary Arts, New York, NY*

½ cup goji berries, soaked until soft
2½ cups frozen mango chunks
½ cup young Thai coconut meat
6–8 oranges, juiced
2 pinches cayenne
Pinch sea salt

Blend all of the ingredients together in a high-speed blender on high for 30–40 seconds.

Simple Lemonade
Lisa Montgomery

2 lemons, juiced
Ice
Stevia, agave, or raw honey to taste

Combine in a high-speed blender and enjoy.

> Option: you can add berries such as raspberries or strawberries to the mixture while blending. Also, try dropping several frozen berries in each glass as a garnish: not only do the frozen berries add flavor, but they also help to keep the drink cool and fun. I love anything that adds spark and pizzazz. If adding a couple of frozen berries to your drink makes it sunshiney, then do it.

Summer Kale
Raw Chef Dan, Quintessence, New York, NY, and Crucina, Madrid, Spain

4 cucumbers, juiced
¼ bunch kale
¼ bunch basil
½ bunch mint
2 yellow squashes
1 clove garlic
1 teaspoon sea salt

Combine the ingredients in a high-speed blender and enjoy.

Watermelon Juice

Lisa Montgomery

I make this all year round. In the summer, it is cool and refreshing, and in the winter, I typically enjoy a glass of watermelon juice after Pilates, because it helps to replace liquids. A lot of healing centers use watermelon juice as part of their basic diet because of its health benefits. In the winter, organic watermelons are hard to find where I live so I buy conventional when I can't find organic. Sometimes, I also juice cantaloupe with the watermelon for a different taste, which also makes the juice creamier.

1 watermelon (red meat only)

Remove the red melon from the skin and juice in a high-speed blender. Store in a sealed glass jar.

Coco-watermelon

Lisa Montgomery

Both watermelon and young Thai coconuts are so good for you and I love them both. So, one day, I decided to combine them in a blender to see what it would taste like. It tasted great.

1 watermelon (red meat)
1 young Thai coconut (meat and juice)

Blend together in a high-speed blender, chill, and serve.

Sweet Peach

*Victoria Boutenko, The Raw Family, author of many books such as
Green for Life and The 12 Steps to Raw Food*

*Victoria has written countless books, travels the world, lectures, and is a
champion of healthy living.*

¼ cup pineapple
¼ cup spinach
2 ripe peaches
½ cup water

Combine all the ingredients in your Tribest Personal blender (or
any high-speed blender). If using a Vitamix®, you can double this
recipe.

If you ever get an opportunity to read one of the Boutenkos' books or attend
any of their workshops or lectures, it will be well worth your time. They are
extremely knowledgeable, intelligent, and delightful. In short, they are just
really nice people. I was so honored to have Victoria and her daughter Valya
speak at one of my raw potlucks several years ago.

Kale-doscope

Victoria Boutenko, The Raw Family, author of many books such as
Green for Life *and* The 12 Steps to Raw Food

½ cup water
¼ cup kale
¼ cup fresh or frozen blueberries
1 golden kiwi
¼ mango

Combine all the ingredients in your Tribest Personal blender (or any high-speed blender). If using a Vitamix®, you can double this recipe.

Pink Dream

Victoria Boutenko, The Raw Family, author of many books such as
Green for Life *and* The 12 Steps to Raw Food

½-¾ cup fresh raspberries
2 ripe kiwis
¾ cup spinach
½ cup water

Combine all the ingredients in your Tribest Personal blender (or any high-speed blender). If using a Vitamix®, you can double this recipe.

Wildly Delicious

Victoria Boutenko, The Raw Family, author of many books such as
Green for Life *and* The 12 Steps to Raw Food

¼ cup orange juice
¼-½ cup dandelion greens
¼ pineapple
¼ mango
½ cup water

Combine all the ingredients in your Tribest Personal blender (or any high-speed blender). If using a Vitamix®, you can double this recipe.

Creamy and Sweet

Victoria Boutenko, The Raw Family, author of many books such as
Green for Life *and* The 12 Steps to Raw Food

½ cup kale
½ banana
½ pear
¾ cup water

Combine all the ingredients in your Tribest Personal blender (or any high-speed blender). If using a Vitamix®, you can double this recipe.

Everyone's Favorite

Victoria Boutenko, The Raw Family, author of many books such as
Green for Life *and* The 12 Steps to Raw Food

½ cup fresh or frozen strawberries
½ banana
½ cup spinach
½ cup mango
½ cup water

Combine all the ingredients in your Tribest Personal blender (or any high-speed blender). If using a Vitamix®, you can double this recipe.

Savory Immune System Booster

Victoria Boutenko, The Raw Family, author of many books such as
Green for Life *and* The 12 Steps to Raw Food

½ cup basil
½ cup cilantro
1 medium tomato
½ avocado
½ cup water
2 cloves garlic
1 tablespoon cayenne pepper
Pinch dulse or sea salt

Combine all the ingredients in your Tribest Personal blender (or any high-speed blender). If using a Vitamix®, you can double this recipe.

Fresh Orange Juice
Lisa Montgomery

4 medium oranges (approximately 8 ounces juiced)

Place oranges in a Tribest Citristar (or any juicer) and juice. Drink and enjoy.

Pear-Cucumber-Mint
Joel Odhner, Transforming People's Relationship to Food, Catalyst Elixir and Raw Food Bar, Philadelphia, PA (www.catalystcleanse.com)

4 pears
1 cucumber
1 ounce mint juice

Run the ingredients through your juicer and enjoy.

Super Cool Cacao Elixir

*Joel Odhner, Transforming People's Relationship to Food, Catalyst Elixir
and Raw Food Bar, Philadelphia, PA (www.catalystcleanse.com)*

1 young Thai coconut (meat and water)
1 tablespoon hemp
2 tablespoons cacao
1 tablespoon goji berries
1 tablespoon maca
½ teaspoon mint extract
1 teaspoon methylsulfonylmethane (MSM)
Pinch sea salt

Combine the above in a high-speed blender until well-blended.

Morning Pick Me Up

Lisa Montgomery

Prep: 15 minutes

4 carrots
2 apples
1 pear
2 oranges
1 lemon

Run the above ingredients together through your Tribest Green-Star juicer. Cool and refreshing!

Good Vibrations

Sheryll Chavarria, Raw Can Roll Café and Pure Body Spa,
Douglassville, PA (www.rawcanrollcafe.com)

Yields 24-ounce drink

2 leaves kale (remove leaves from stem)
½ apple
1 stalk celery
12 ounces water
Handful cucumber (optional)
½ banana (optional)
1 thin slice lemon with rind (optional, to help slow down
    oxidation)

Place ingredients in a high-speed blender and blend well.

Kata Bay Delight
(Thai Pineapple-Lime Delight)

*Raw Chef Dan, Quintessence, New York, NY, and Crucina,
Madrid, Spain*

*This drink is so exotic and wonderful, and is inspired by Thailand's
beautiful Kata bay near the southern tip of Phuket.*

1 cup ice, crushed
1 ripe banana
1½-inch ring fresh pineapple
1 large kaffir lime leaf
8 ounces young Thai coconut water
⅛ teaspoon sea salt

Combine the ingredients in a high-speed blender.

If available, star fruit is a nice addition to this drink.

You can order kaffir lime from Amazon.com.

Another One of Lisa's Favorite Green Juices

Lisa Montgomery

2 cucumbers
4 celery stalks
½–1 cup sunflower sprouts
3 pears
1 lemon (juice only)

Run all the ingredients through the juicer. Drink and enjoy.

Strawberry Fields

Susan Barrett, Rob Nagy, Strawberry Fields Juice and Smoothie Bar,
Phoenixville, PA

Yield: 12 ounces juice (juicing removes all skin and fiber)

1½ apples, cut into quarters with stem removed, or 6 ounces
    apple juice
Handful mint leaves, juiced with apple
1 cup strawberries

Alternate fruit through the juicer, and then whisk in a cup to combine the ingredients.

We Got the Beet

Susan Barrett, Roby Nagy, Strawberry Fields Juice and Smoothie Bar,
Phoenixville, PA

Yield: 12 ounces blended juice

1 apple (4 ounces)
1 beet
⅛ lime
1 large kale leaf

Juice together the apple, beet, and lime into a large measuring cup.
Pour into a blender pitcher. Add 1 large kale leaf and blend into
juice.

A blended juice involves juicing a fruit or vegetable, and then
blending in another fruit or vegetable in order to maintain
some of the fiber.

SOUPS

People who are not familiar with the raw lifestyle often cringe at the thought of eating cold soup, but keep in mind that raw soups can be served chilled, at room temperature, or warmed (but not any higher than 118°F). If you don't have a food thermometer to check the temperature, you can simply use your finger: if you warm the soup so it feels warm to your finger, it should be less than 118°F. I have also used my slow-cooker on the lowest setting to warm my soups. If you use a high-speed blender and you blend long enough, the process will also warm your soup as well. When I use the slow-cooker, I have been known to combine vegetables that I have dehydrated myself or purchased from Heritage Creek Farm, along with fresh mushroom, a pint of corn, and tomatoes that I froze along with some seasonings. I then simply let it all simmer for several hours. One of the many beautiful features of living the raw lifestyle is, even when making soup, you can combine whatever vegetables that you have with your favorite seasoning and come up with a fabulous soup. It is that simple.

Vegetable Soup

Brenda Cobb, founder of Living Foods Institute and author of The Living Foods Lifestyle, *Atlanta, GA*

Prep: 20 minutes

Soup Base
1 red, yellow, or orange bell pepper
9 very ripe roma tomatoes
3 stalks celery
⅔ cup water
1 teaspoon Celtic sea salt
2 teaspoon dried oregano
Pinch cayenne pepper

Vegetables
2 roma tomatoes, chopped
½ cup celery, chopped
½ cup red pepper, chopped
½ zucchini or yellow squash

Soup Base
Blend all the ingredients in a Vitamix® blender until creamy. Remove and put in a bowl.

Vegetables
Chop the vegetables into very small bite-size pieces. Combine the chopped vegetables with the soup and enjoy.

Almond Creamy Soup Base for 100 Soups

Rhio, Hooked on Raw

This is a fantastic soup base that can be used to create numerous wonderful soups.

Prep: 20 minutes
Sprout: almonds, 24 hours

1½ cups raw almonds, sprouted
2 cups filtered water
2 lemons, juiced
1 clove garlic
1 tablespoon flaxseed oil
½ teaspoon ground cumin
½ teaspoon Celtic sea salt
Dash Nama Shoyu (optional)

Place all the ingredients in a high-speed blender and blend very well.

See pages 74 and 75 for variations on this soup base.

Lemon-Zucchini Bisque

Rhio, Hooked on Raw

Almond Creamy Soup Base (page 73)

2 small zucchinis, grated
½ cup shallot or onion, finely minced
1 ear corn, cut off the cob
¼ cup shallot, finely minced
¼ red bell pepper, finely chopped
2 mushrooms, finely chopped

Place all the ingredients in a high-speed blender and blend very well.

Almond-Beet Borscht

Rhio, Hooked on Raw

Almond Creamy Soup Base (page 73)

½ beet, grated
½ cup cucumber, chopped
¼ cup chives, finely minced
Sprinkle dill, chopped

Place all the ingredients in a high-speed blender and blend very well.

Creamy Spinach Swirl

Rhio, Hooked on Raw

Serves 2–4
Almond Creamy Soup Base (page 73)

½ bunch spinach
½ teaspoon garam masala

Divide the soup base in half. Put ½ back into the blender with spinach and garam masala, and blend well. Pour the white soup base into 2–4 soup bowls, and then pour the green-spinach blend into each bowl. Using a spoon, stir gently. It will swirl out and look like the colors in a Matisse painting: beautiful and delicious. Because of the spices, this soup will keep for 2 days in the refrigerator.

Beetroot Gazpacho

Bearnairdin Ni Goibniu, The Little House of Avalon, Quantum
Wellness and Holistic Retreat, Ireland

Prep: 25 minutes

1 kilogram ripe plum tomatoes
1 small onion, chopped
1 small green pepper, cut into small chunks
1 clove garlic
1 small white potato
5 tablespoons extra virgin olive oil
3 tablespoons sherry vinegar
1 tablespoon horseradish (optional)
2 beetroots, peeled and chopped
1 Granny Smith apple
1 avocado
Himalayan sea salt and ground pepper to taste

Combine tomatoes, onion, pepper, garlic, and potato in a food processor with an S-blade, and then process until the mixture is pureed. While the processor is running, slowly add the oil until the blend thickens and forms an emulsion. Add vinegar, horseradish, and beetroot, blend well, and season to taste. Flavor should be slightly sour and sweet. Chill overnight.

Pour soup into bowls. Peel the apple and shred it into fine strips. Place some creamed avocado on the soup and garnish with the apple shreds.

Arugula Pear Soup

Raw Chef Dan, Quintessence, New York, NY, and Crucina,
Madrid, Spain

Prep: 25 minutes

2 cups arugula, chopped
1 cup water
1 medium cucumber, chopped
1 stalk celery, chopped
1 pear, stem removed and chopped
3 tablespoons red onion, minced
3 tablespoons fresh lemon juice
2 tablespoons cold-pressed olive oil
1½ teaspoons sea salt
2 teaspoons Austria's Finest Naturally® Pumpkin Seed Oil
       (optional)

Blend ingredients together in a high-speed blender until creamy.

Bell Pepper Soup

Raw Chef Dan, Quintessence, New York, NY, and Crucina,
Madrid, Spain

Prep: 25 minutes

3 cups filtered water
¼ cup cold-pressed olive oil
1 teaspoon sea salt
1 teaspoon caraway seeds
2 medium cloves garlic
2 medium red or yellow bell peppers (discarding the green
    stems)
2 medium cucumbers, chopped
½ medium red onion, chopped

Blend ingredients in a high-speed blender until creamy and
smooth.

Butternut Comfort Soup

Tonya Zavasta, author of Beautiful on Raw: unCooked Creations
(www.beautifulonraw.com)

Serves approximately 2
Prep: 25 minutes

Meat of 1 young Thai coconut
1 cup coconut water
1 cup butternut squash, peeled and cubed
4 soaked dates (or ¼ cup another raw natural sweetener)
Dash cinnamon and nutmeg

Blend the ingredients at high speed until smooth. If desired, serve garnished with grated apple or more coconut.

Carrot-Ginger Soup

Janice Innella, The Beauty Chef

Prep: 30 minutes

4 cups carrots, chopped

1 cup water

1 pear

1 young Thai coconut (meat and water)

3 tablespoons coconut butter and/or oil

2-inch piece fresh ginger, peeled

1 teaspoon ginger powder

1 shallot

4 ounces raw cashews

1 tablespoon agave nectar

1 teaspoon garam masala

⅛ teaspoon ground coriander

1 pinch each cloves, nutmeg, black pepper, and cinnamon

Blend all of the above ingredients together. Garnish with pumpkin seed oil and chives on top. Serve at room temperature.

Coconut Thai Soup

Raw Chef Dan, Quintessence, New York, NY, and Crucina, Madrid Spain

Prep: 20 minutes

1 whole young Thai Coconut (meat and water)
2 cups water
½ cup coconut flakes
1 1-inch piece ginger
3 kaffir lime leaves
1 medium clove garlic
1 tablespoon coconut butter
¼ teaspoon sea salt
1 teaspoon soy sauce
½ lime, juiced
Thai chili to taste

Blend all of the above together in a high-speed blender.

Cucumber-Avocado Soup

Raw Chef Dan, Quintessence, New York, NY, and Crucina, Madrid Spain

Prep: 15 minutes

1 large cucumber, chopped
1 cup water
1 stalk celery
¼ Hass avocado
1 tablespoon fresh dill, chopped
1 tablespoon fresh lemon juice

Combine all of the above in a high-speed blender.

Cucumber-Pineapple Gazpacho

Joel Odhner, Catalyst Cleanse, Rawlife Line, Philadelphia, PA

Prep: 30 minutes

4 cups cucumber, chopped and peeled
4 cups pineapple, chopped
1 small jalapeño pepper, seeded and diced
1 green onion, chopped
1 tablespoon lime juice
2 teaspoons sea salt
Handful cilantro leaves
2 tablespoons cold-pressed virgin olive oil

Place all the ingredients in a food processor or high-speed blender and blend. Chill and enjoy.

Energy Soup

Elaina Love, author of Elaina's Pure Joy Kitchen,
www.purejoyplanet.com

Prep: 35 minutes
Makes 4 cups

Step 1

1½ cups water

½ small yam

1 medium carrot or equal amount butternut squash, cut into
    chunks

1 Golden Delicious or other sweet apple, cut into chunks

½ small onion and/or 1 clove garlic (garlic will make it spicy)

Small handful dulse or wakame or ½ teaspoon kelp powder

Step 2

1 medium zucchini, chopped

½ stalk celery, chopped

3–4 fresh basil leaves

Step 3

2 handfuls sunflower, buckwheat, or pea sprouts or baby greens

1 avocado, chopped

3 tablespoons Bragg Liquid Aminos, Nama Shoyu Living Soy
    Sauce, or ½-1 teaspoon Celtic sea salt

½ teaspoon cumin powder

½ teaspoon garlic powder (optional)

½ teaspoon onion powder (optional)

Place all the ingredients in Step 1 into the blender and mix for 30
seconds.

Add ingredients from Step 2 and blend for 30 more seconds.

Add the remainder of the ingredients and blend until creamy (just long enough so everything is well-blended).

Add the garlic and onion powder only after tasting and deciding if the soup needs more spice.

You can also top with:

- Chopped red bell peppers
- Fresh corn off the cob
- Chunks of avocado
- Dehydrated crackers broken into pieces

Butternut Squash or Sweet Potato Soup

Elaina Love, author of Elaina's Pure Joy Kitchen,
www.purejoyplanet.com

Prep: 25 minutes
Makes 6 cups

2 cups water (plus more, if needed)

¾ small butternut squash, peeled and sliced, or 2 small sweet
 potatoes, peeled and cubed

1 yellow or orange bell pepper, chopped (save ½ for garnish)

2 stalks celery

½ red onion

3 basil leaves

½ cup tahini or almond butter

½ teaspoon curry powder

1 teaspoon cumin

⅛ teaspoon nutmeg

½ teaspoon garlic powder or clove fresh garlic

3 tablespoons Bragg Liquid Aminos or ½-1 teaspoon Celtic sea
 salt

1 medium-to-large avocado (optional for a creamier texture)

2 scallions, minced (for garnish)

Blend water and squash (or potatoes) for 1 minute in a high-speed
blender.

   Add the remaining ingredients (except avocado, scallions, and
½ of the bell pepper). Blend another 40 seconds or so.

   Add the avocado and blend until creamy. Garnish with scallions and chopped bell pepper.

Curried Creamy Mushroom Soup

Tribest, Home of the Green Star Juicer and Sedona Dehydrator

This recipe is from the folks at Tribest and is designed to be made in their Soyabella. Besides making soup in my Soyabella, I also use it to make almond milk.

Prep: 30 minutes

1 cup Sun Jewels Organics curried cashews
1 cup mushrooms, sliced
1 teaspoon pepper
Water
1 teaspoon poultry spice blend
1 teaspoon sea salt
Pinch curry powder
Raw butter or cold-pressed olive oil
Fresh parsley for garnish

Place cashews, mushrooms, and pepper into Soyabella's stainless-steel chamber. Add enough water to reach the 0.8-liter mark. Follow the instructions for making creamy/pureed soup from the Soyabella directions sheet. Mix in the poultry spice, sea salt, curry powder, and pat of raw butter or cold-pressed olive oil. Garnish with minced parsley.

Tribest's original recipe calls for a pat of butter, which I have replaced with cold-pressed olive oil because I am allergic to dairy, and dairy is not generally part of the raw lifestyle.

Raw Raw for Squash Soup

Tribest

This recipe is from the folks at Tribest and is designed to be made in their Soyabella.

Prep: 25 minutes

2 cups mushrooms, sliced
1 cup Sun Jewels Organics curried cashews
8 ounces water
1 teaspoon poultry spice
1–2 teaspoons soy sauce
1 teaspoon sea salt
½ cup raw zucchini, grated for each serving

Place the mushrooms, curried cashews, and poultry spice into the Soyabella's stainless-steel chamber. Add enough water to reach the 0.8-liter mark. Follow the instructions for making creamy/pureed soup. Mix in the soy sauce, sea salt, and cold-pressed olive oil (I substitute this, whereas Tribest calls for a pat of butter). Serve warm, adding the raw grated zucchini last (½ cup for each 8 ounces of soup broth).

Creamy Mushroom Soup with Parsley Garnish

Sheryll Chavarria, Raw Can Roll Café and Pure Body Spa,
Douglassville, PA (www.rawcanrollcafe.com)

Prep: 20 minutes

2 cups almond milk
½ cup celery
2 cups mushrooms
1 tablespoon tahini
1 teaspoon cold-pressed olive oil (optional)
¼ cup parsley or scallions, finely chopped (for garnish)
1 tablespoon white miso (or to taste)

Place all the ingredients into a high-speed blender and blend until lightly creamy, being careful not to over-blend. Serve in bowls and garnish with parsley or finely chopped scallions.

Curried Carrot-Avocado Soup

Joel Odhner, Catalyst Cleanse, Rawlife Line, Philadelphia, PA

Prep: 25 minutes

3 cups carrots, chopped

2 cups water

2 avocados, peeled and seeded

1 clove garlic, minced

¼ inch ginger root, peeled and chopped

1 teaspoon curry

1 teaspoon cumin

Pinch sea salt

Pinch cayenne

Blend the above ingredients in a high-speed blender or food processor until smooth.

Sexy Gazpacho

Karmyn Malone (www.karmynmalone.com)

Prep: 20 minutes
Serves 2 sexy people

4 cups grape or red cherry tomatoes (or Campari or other
       premium tomatoes), halved or quartered
½ cup red bell pepper
8 sun-dried tomato halves, soaked and drained
2 tablespoons raw honey or raw agave nectar
2 handfuls fresh basil
Thai red pepper (½ pepper or more to taste)

Add all the ingredients to a high-speed blender in the order listed.

Pour gazpacho into 2 serving bowls. Garnish with chopped, peeled cucumber and some fresh basil.

> If using a Vitamix® blender, I recommend using the slowest 2 speeds. Otherwise, you will end up with a "Sexy Marinara Sauce" instead of Sexy Gazpacho.
>
> Make sure to push down the ingredients in the blender with the tamper. This recipe works best in a high-powered blender like the Vitamix®. If using a regular blender, use a celery stalk to push the ingredients down.

South of the Border Gazpacho

Karmyn Malone (www.karmynmalone.com)

Serves 2
Prep: 20 minutes

4 cups Campari or other fine tomatoes, halved or quartered
1 cup red bell pepper, sliced
2 medium celery stalks
8 sun-dried tomatoes, halved, soaked, and drained
2 tablespoon raw honey or raw agave
2 handfuls fresh cilantro
½ jalapeño pepper (more or less to taste)

Add all the ingredients to a high-speed blender in the order listed.

Pour gazpacho into 2 serving bowls. Garnish with chopped, peeled cucumber and some fresh chopped cilantro.

If using a Vitamix® blender, I recommend using the slowest 2 speeds. Otherwise, you will end up with a marinara sauce instead of gazpacho.

Make sure to push down the ingredients in the blender with the tamper. This recipe works best in a high-powered blender like the Vitamix®. If using a regular blender, use a celery stalk to push the ingredients down.

Joel's Gazpacho

Joel Odhner, Catalyst Cleanse, Rawlife Line, Philadelphia, PA

Prep: 30 minutes

5 cups vine-ripened tomatoes, diced
¼ cup cold-pressed extra virgin olive oil
1 jalapeño, seeded and diced (optional)
Dash cumin
3 cucumbers, seeded and cubed
Bunch cilantro, chopped
Handful mint, chopped
3 tablespoons fresh lime juice
Celtic sea salt to taste

Place tomatoes, olive oil, jalapeño, and spices in a food processor or high-powered blender, and blend until the desired consistency. Mix in cucumbers, cilantro, and mint. Chill. Add lime juice before serving.

Gazpacho was brought to the United States from the Andalusia region of Spain. Gazpacho combines chopped or pureed produce such as tomatoes, cucumbers, onions, peppers, and celery. It can be spicy or milky, and is seasoned with herbs, garlic, olive oil, hot peppers, and vinegar or citrus juice. Because of the strong ingredients (such as raw garlic, onion, herbs, and spices), it is recommended that you keep it in the refrigerator for a few hours to allow the flavors to mellow by serving time. Gazpacho is similar to hummus or guacamole in that everyone has their favorite version. In this book, I have shared with you several of my favorite gazpachos.

Holiday Gazpacho Soup

Frederic Patenaude's New Year's Day Menu (www.fredericpatenaude. com)

Prep: 25 minutes

3 tomatoes, chopped
½ red pepper, chopped
½ yellow pepper, chopped
¼ small zucchini
¼ cucumber
2 tablespoons red onion
½ cup corn (optional)
¼ cup cilantro, chopped
1 clove garlic, mashed (optional)
1 tablespoon lime juice
Pinch cayenne

Blend half of the ingredients in a high-speed blender until smooth; then add the remaining ingredients and pulse chop until they are finely chopped. Alternatively, you may pulse or chop half of the ingredients in a food processor, and then add to the soup base and stir. Pour into a bowl and enjoy. Gazpacho can be stored in the refrigerator for 2 days.

New York Gazpacho

Raw Chef Dan, Quintessence, New York, NY, and Crucina, Madrid, Spain

Prep: 35 minutes

3 cups tomato, chopped
1 cup cucumber, chopped
¼ cup fresh cilantro
¼ cup fresh parsley
2 tablespoons lime juice
2 tablespoons lemon juice
1 large clove garlic, minced
1 teaspoon sea salt

Blend the above ingredients in a food processor with the S-blade. Fully blend without making a puree out of the mixture.

Moroccan Tomato Ginger Soup

Raw Chef Dan, Quintessence, New York, NY, and Crucina,
Madrid, Spain

Prep: 30 minutes

3 tomatoes
¼ cup sun-dried tomatoes
4 ounces ginger, minced
½ cup tahini
1 teaspoon cardamom
1 teaspoon cumin
1 teaspoon caraway
1 teaspoon cumin
2 cloves garlic, finely chopped
¼ cup basil, chopped
¼ cup parsley, chopped
¼ cup cold-pressed olive oil
1 teaspoon sea salt

Combine all of the ingredients in a high-speed blender until smooth. I drizzle the top with the typical tahini-garlic-lemon dressing.

Pumpkin Bisque

Raw Chef Dan, Quintessence, New York, NY, and Crucina, Madrid, Spain

Prep: 30 minutes

3 cups pumpkin, peeled and chopped into 1-by-1-inch cubes
2 cups water
½ cup pine nuts
¼ small red onion
1 medium red or yellow bell pepper
Juice ½ lemon
2 tablespoons cold-pressed olive oil
¼ teaspoon nutmeg
1 teaspoon fresh oregano
1 teaspoon sea salt

In a high-speed blender, blend the pumpkin with the remaining ingredients.

> If you buy the pumpkin already peeled and cut, it shortens your preparation time considerably.

Pineapple Soup

Joel Odhner, Catalyst Cleanse, Rawlife Line, Philadelphia, PA

I love this soup. The pineapple and cucumber make it so cool and refreshing.

Prep: 20 minutes

1 pineapple, cubed with skin removed
1–2 cucumbers
1 jalapeño (optional)
¼ cup lime juice
Pinch sea salt
¼ cup cold-pressed olive oil
⅛ cup onion, chopped

Blend together the ingredients in a high-speed blender and serve.

Pumpkin Coconut Masala Soup

Janice Innella, The Beauty Chef

Prep: 30 minutes

1 butternut squash or 3–4 cups zucchini
2 young Thai coconuts (juice and meat)
3 tablespoons Austria's Finest Naturally® Pumpkin Seed Oil
3 dates, pitted
1 teaspoon cinnamon
⅛ teaspoon nutmeg
⅛ teaspoon clove
1 teaspoon cardamom
1 vanilla bean or 1 tablespoon alcohol-free vanilla extract
½ cup raw cashews
2 tablespoons raw honey or agave nectar, or ½ cup dates, pitted

Blend all of the ingredients together in a high-speed blender until creamy. Serve with a drizzle of pumpkin seed oil on top.

Spinach Basil Soup

Raw Chef Dan, Quintetssence, New York, NY, and Crucina,
Madrid, Spain

Prep: 30 minutes

4 cups water
1 bunch spinach, chopped to fit in blender
½ bunch basil (or about 2 cups, loosely packed)
¼ small red onion, chopped
1 medium cucumber, chopped
1 medium tomato, chopped
2 stalks celery, chopped
¼ cup pine nuts
¼ cup cold-pressed olive oil
1 medium clove garlic, minced
1 teaspoon sea salt
Pinch cayenne (optional)

Combine all of the above ingredients together in a high-speed blender until smooth.

Raw Tomato Soup

Rhonda Malkmus, Hallelujah Acres, Shelby, NC

Prep: 15 minutes

2 cups vine-ripe tomatoes
1 stalk celery
1 fresh basil leaf
1 inch fresh oregano leaves on stem
1 garlic/chive spike

Place all ingredients in a Vitamix® or other high-speed blender. Push all the ingredients into the blades with the plunger. Turn the blender on high until all the ingredients are thoroughly pulverized. Pour into mugs and serve.

Options: you can add finely chopped sweet onion and red pepper to the soup after it is removed from the blender.

Tomato-Seafood Stew

Raw Chef Dan, Quintessence, New York, NY, and Crucina,
Madrid, Spain

Prep: 30 minutes
Presoak: hiziki, 2 hours (minimum)

2 ounces hiziki per serving

3 cups water

5 sun-dried tomatoes, soaked until soft

¼ cup dulse

¼ cup loose basil

3 tablespoons cold-pressed olive oil

1 tablespoon fresh dill, minced

1 tablespoon fresh oregano, minced

1 large clove garlic, minced

2 tablespoons lemon juice

2 teaspoon sea salt

Pine nuts (for garnish)

Capers (for garnish)

Presoak hiziki for a minimum of 2 hours and set aside. Blend all the ingredients (except hiziki, pine nuts, and capers) in a high-speed blender. When serving, place 4 ounces of soup, 2 ounces of soaked hiziki, 1 ounce of pine nuts, and 1 spoon of capers into each bowl. Drizzle with a few drops of oil and a dash of paprika.

Zuppa Del Giorno Creamed Celery Root

Janice Innella, The Beauty Chef

Soup
Prep: 30 minutes

Shitake Garnish
Dehydrate: 6 to 8 hours at 105 °F

Soup
1 medium celery root, peeled and cleaned
2 cloves garlic, minced
3 tablespoons cold-pressed olive oil
1 teaspoon Celtic sea salt
1 cup cashews
2 cups seaweed water (soak kombu)
1 tablespoon Nama Shoyu

Shitake Garnish
1 tablespoon Nama Shoyu
1 cup shitake mushrooms, sliced thinly
½ cup golden flaxseeds, ground
1 lemon, juiced
1 bunch chives (for garnish)

Soup
Combine all the ingredients together in a high-speed blender until creamy. Set aside in serving bowls.

Shitake Garnish
Marinade all the ingredients and roll in ground flax. Place on dehydrator at 105°F and dehydrate for 6–8 hours (you will need to make this the day before or the morning before serving your soup).

Watercress-Pear Soup

Potlucker Mary Kane

Prep: 25 minutes
Soak: nuts, 4–6 hours

2 pears
½ cup pecans, soaked
⅔–1 tablespoon allspice
2 tablespoons pumpkin seed oil
½ bunch watercress
¼ cup cold-pressed olive oil
1 cup filtered water
Sea salt to taste

Blend all of the ingredients together in a high-speed blender to desired consistency.

Some folks like this soup creamy and smooth, while others like the pear chunky and the watercress chopped so it is more visible. See what works best for you.

Un-Chicken Noodle Soup

Victoria Boutenko, The Raw Family, *author of many books such as*
Green for Life *and* The 12 Steps to Raw Food

Serves 7
Prep: 25 minutes

2 cups water
½ cup coconut, shredded and un-sulphered
2 cups celery, chopped
2 tablespoons Bragg Liquid Aminos
1 clove garlic
1 medium carrot, grated
¼ bunch parsley, chopped
2 medium raw potatoes, grated or processed with spiralizer
Mushrooms, sliced (optional)
Pepper to taste (if desired)

Blend together the water and coconut very well for 1–2 minutes in
a high-speed blender. Add the celery, Bragg Liquid Aminos, garlic,
and pepper, and then blend for about 1 minute. Pour into a large
bowl and add the remaining ingredients.

Generic Recipe for Chowder

Victoria Boutenko, The Raw Family, author of many books such as
Green for Life *and* The 12 Steps to Raw Food

Serves 5

1 cup coconut
2 cups water, divided
1 cup cashews
½ cup extra virgin olive oil
1 teaspoon honey
1 cup celery, chopped
2–5 cloves garlic
Hot peppers to taste

Blend the coconut with 1 cup of water for 1 minute in a high-speed blender or 2 minutes in a regular blender. Add cashews and blend for another 30 seconds. Add the remaining ingredients with another cup of water and blend well. Sprinkle with dry parsley flakes before serving.

This recipe is for plain chowder. Here are some flavors that you can add:

> For clam-chowder: add dulce flakes

> For broccoli: add chopped broccoli

> For mushroom: add your favorite mushroom, dry or fresh

> For tomato: add chopped tomato

- For carrots: add grated carrots

- For corn: add corn, cut off the cob (or use frozen corn)

- For pea soup: add fresh or frozen peas

> This soup will become warm because of so much blending, but it is still raw (just don't let it become hot). Warm soups are comforting in the cold winter time.

DRESSINGS, SAUCES, AND DIPS

It is amazing how adding a dressing or sauce can take a salad from average to "wow." These dressings and sauces will make your salads pop. In fact, they are so good that you may forgo the salad and just eat the dressing. Dips for me are just plain comfort: there is something about the hand-to-mouth movement that nourishes me physically and emotionally. Some of my meals have been accomplished by just dipping celery and carrot sticks into a great dip or spreading the dip on a cracker. I sometimes also like to combine dips, sauces, and dressings in a collard wrap with vegetable sticks to make an amazing meal.

Almond-Tahini Dressing

*Raw Chef Dan, Quintessence, New York, NY, and Crucina,
Madrid, Spain*

Makes 2½ cups

8 ounces raw organic sesame tahini
4 ounces raw almond butter
Juice ½ medium organic lemon
2 medium cloves garlic
¼ teaspoon Celtic sea salt or Himalayan crystal salt
1 cup filtered or spring water
1 teaspoon fresh dill, chopped (optional)

Place all of the ingredients together in a high-speed blender until
smooth.

Traditional Ranch Dressing

Sheryll Chavarria, Raw Can Roll Café and Pure Body Spa,
Douglassville, PA (www.rawcanrollcafe.com)

2 cups cashews, soaked
Water (as needed)
1 teaspoon lemon juice
½ tablespoon onion powder
½ tablespoon garlic powder
¼ cup dill
¼ cup parsley
Sea salt to taste

Blend all the ingredients (except dill and parsley) together in a high-speed blender. Then add the herbs for a very light blend (you do not want the dressing to turn green; you just want flecks of green).

Dipping Sauce

Lisa Montgomery

This is a great dipping sauce for bok choy, celery, collard roll-ups, or zucchini roll-ups. It also makes a great dressing.

1–2 cloves garlic, chopped
1 tablespoon ginger, grated
4 tablespoons water
4 tablespoons wheat-free tamari
2 tablespoons cold-pressed olive oil or sesame oil
1–2 dates
2 tablespoons sesame tahini
Dash pepper
Dash curry
Dash sea salt

Using a small blender (or mix by hand), blend all of the ingredients together.

Creamy Herb Dressing

Raw Chef Dan, Quintessence, New York, NY, and Crucina,
Madrid, Spain

Prep: 15 minutes

1 cup water
1 cup raw cashews or macadamia nuts
¼ cup cold-pressed olive oil
2 tablespoons lemon juice
1 teaspoon sea salt
1 large date, pitted
1 tablespoon oregano, chopped
1 tablespoon basil, chopped
1 tablespoon sage, chopped
1 tablespoon dill, chopped

Combine the water, raw nuts, olive oil, lemon juice, salt, and date in a high-speed blender and blend on high speed. Then add the herbs to the blender and run at medium speed. Combine the herbs, but do not blend completely.

Japanese House Dressing

Raw Chef Dan, Quintessence, New York, NY, and Crucina,
Madrid, Spain

Prep: 20 minutes

2 cups water
1 cup yam, chopped
1 cup lemon juice
1 cup white miso
1 cup white onion, chopped
½ cup raw tahini
½ cup ginger, chopped
3 tablespoons Nama Shoyu
1½ teaspoons agave
½ cup yam, chopped

Blend all of the ingredients (except yam) together in a high-speed blender. Blend until smooth. Then add the yam, run the blender on medium speed, and chop the dressing until it is slightly grainy.

Caesar Dressing

Brenda Cobb, founder of Living Foods Institute and author of The Living Foods Lifestyle

Prep: 10 minutes

3 large cloves garlic
⅔ cup lemon juice
⅔ cup olive oil
3 tablespoons dulse seaweed flakes
1 teaspoon Himalayan sea salt

Mince the garlic very fine and combine with the lemon juice, olive oil, dulse, and sea salt. Place dressing mixture in a glass jar, cover, and shake well.

Wait until right before you are ready to serve this and toss with romaine salad greens, completely coating all the leaves.

Serve and feast.

Tomato-Pepper Dressing

Brenda Cobb, founder of Living Foods Institute and author of
The Living Foods Lifestyle

5 medium roma tomatoes (if small, use 8)
1 large clove garlic
12 red, yellow, or orange bell peppers
2 tablespoons lemon juice
½ teaspoon Celtic or Himalayan sea salt
1 tablespoon olive oil
2 tablespoons water

Blend the ingredients together in a Vitamix® blender until creamy.

Be sure to remove the green stem from the red pepper. Save all of the red part and the seeds.

Cucumber, Yogurt, and Dill Dressing

Jackie Graff, RN BSN (http://rawfoodrevial.com)

1 cup raw macadamia nuts, soaked overnight and drained
¼ cup lemon juice
1 cup raw pine nuts, soaked overnight and drained
6–8 cucumbers, peeled and chopped
2 teaspoons sea salt
1 cup fresh dill, chopped fine
3 cloves garlic

Blend together all the ingredients (except dill) in a high-speed blender. Add the dill after the dressing is well-blended. This dressing will keep for 3–5 days in the refrigerator.

French Delight Dressing

Jackie Graff, RN BSN (http://rawfoodrevial.com)

2 medjool dates, pitted and soaked in ½ cup filtered water

⅓ cup sun-dried tomatoes, soaked in 1 cup filtered water

1 clove garlic

¼ cup unpasteurized apple cider vinegar

¼ cup cold-pressed olive oil

2 teaspoons tamari

½ teaspoon sea salt

1 tablespoon paprika

1 teaspoon dry mustard

Place all of the ingredients (including the soaking water) in a high-speed blender and blend well. If too thick, add more filtered water. This dressing will keep for 1 week in the refrigerator.

Raspberry Dressing

Jackie Graff, RN BSN (http://rawfoodrevial.com)

2 cups raspberries

1 cup filtered water

1 tablespoon lemon juice

1 tablespoon lemon zest

6–8 medjool dates, pitted and soaked for 1 hour

1 tablespoon curry powder

½ teaspoon sea salt (optional)

½ cup olive or flax oil (optional: leave out for fat free)

¼ cup tarragon, chopped fine

¼ sweet onion, chopped fine

Place raspberries, water, lemon juice, zest, dates, curry, salt, and oil in a high-speed blender, and blend until smooth. Stir in chopped tarragon and onion.

    This is good served over spinach or romaine and over fruit salads (if not using the oil). Substitute strawberries for a slightly different flavor. This dressing will keep over 3–5 days in the refrigerator.

Raw Tahini

Jackie Graff, RN BSN (http://rawfoodrevial.com)

3 cups sesame seeds, hulled
1¼ cups olive oil or flax oil

Place sesame seeds and oil in a high-speed blender and blend until smooth and creamy. Refrigerate immediately. This may be kept for a month or more.

Thousand Island Dressing

Jackie Graff, RN BSN (http://rawfoodrevial.com)

1 lemon, juiced

1 cup sun-dried tomatoes, soaked in 3 cups filtered water for 1
hour

½ cup pine nuts, soaked in filtered water for 1 hour and drained

3 medjool dates, pitted and soaked in 1 cup filtered water for 1
hour

1 cup pickle juice

3 dill pickles (see page 122), chopped small

Filtered water (to taste and for desired consistency)

Place all the ingredients (except the pickles) in a blender with the
tomato and date soaking water, and blend well to a creamy consistency. If too thick, add more filtered water or pickle juice before
adding the chopped pickles. Pour dressing into a bowl and stir in
the chopped dill pickles.

> If you do not wish to make your own pickles, Bubbies® Raw Dill
> Pickles can be substituted.

Fermented Dill Pickles

Jackie Graff, RN BSN (http://rawfoodrevial.com)

½ cup sea salt
1 gallon distilled water
¼ cup pickling spices
3 cloves garlic, crushed
1 teaspoon dill seed
1 large bunch dill weed, washed
3 pounds pickling cucumbers, washed with filtered water
3 probiotic capsules (8–10 or more different lactic bacteria)

Combine the salt and water in a pitcher and stir until the salt is dissolved. Set aside.

Place the pickling spices, garlic, dill seed, and dill weed into a 1-gallon crock, glass jar, or food-grade plastic container, and add the cucumbers.

Pour the salt water over the cucumbers to completely cover. Open the probiotics, empty them into the water, and mix well.

Pour any remaining salt water in a 1-gallon ziplock bag, and seal to be used as a weight on top of the pickles. Then place this bag on top of the pickles, making sure that they all are submerged in the brine. Cover and set in a cool place.

The pickles should be ready in 3–7 days. Check daily and skim off any scum. The water and the pickles should taste sour. When they are ready, refrigerate in jars with some juice (save the remainder of the juice for fermenting other vegetables). The brine will sometimes become cloudy from the lactic bacteria and white chunks of colonized bacteria may occur, which can simply be skimmed off.

Mushroom Gravy

Joel Odhner, Catalyst Cleanse, Rawlife Line, Philadelphia, PA

1 cup portobello mushrooms, chopped
1 cup olive oil
¼ cup Bragg
¼ cup onion, choppd
½ red pepper, chopped

Place all of the ingredients together in a high-speed blender and blend until smooth. Add just enough water to reach the desired consistency. This dressing will last for 2–3 days in the refrigerator.

Raw Mayo

Jill Santer, author of Breaking Free: Truths For Healthy Living

This is great for mock egg salad, mock tuna salad, potato salad, as a topping on a veggie burger, or as a salad dressing with extra olive oil. You can also add red peppers and carrots to instantly transform this into ranch or French dressing.

1 cup raw cashews
2 young Thai coconuts (meat only)
½ cup pure water
1 teaspoon Celtic sea salt
⅛ teaspoon cayenne
1 teaspoon raw honey or light agave
1 lemon (juice only)
½ cup or more cold-pressed olive oil

Combine all the ingredients (except the oil) together in a high-speed blender and blend. Add the oil slowly.

Pico De Gallo

Frederic Patenaude (www.fredericpateanude.com)

4 cups tomatoes, finely diced

2 limes, diced

¼ cup onions, finely diced

1 cup pineapple, finely diced

1 cup cilantro, chopped

2 tablespoons apple cider vinegar or lemon juice

1 teaspoon cumin

2 tablespoons maple syrup or raw honey (optional)

Combine all the ingredients together in a bowl.

You can experiment by adding other spices if desired, but this recipe is also great as is.

Green Dill Dressing

Frederic Patenaude (www.fredericpatenaude.com)

3 medium tomatoes
6 tablespoons tahini
2 cups spinach
1 orange, juiced
½ cup fresh dill

Blend all the ingredients together in a high-speed blender until smooth. Season, if desired, and serve with your favorite salad.

Mango Dressing

Raw Chef Lynn Devaney

Makes about 1¼ cups

1 cup mango
½ cup water
2 tablespoons lime juice
1 tablespoon agave
½ teaspoon curry powder
⅛ teaspoon red pepper flakes

Combine all the ingredients together in a high-speed blender.

The Little House of Avalon House Dressing

Bearnairdin Ni Goibniu, The Little House of Avalon, Quantum Wellness and Holistic Retreat, Ireland

Prep: 15 minutes

½ cup coconut water
½ cup orange juice
½ cup pine nuts
½ cup strawberries
½ teaspoon agave
1 teaspoon lemon juice
Parsley, chopped (for garnish or optional)
Salt to taste
Black pepper to taste

Blend all the ingredients except parsley. Adjust consistency and taste. Sprinkle in parsley.

PUDDINGS AND SOUFFLÉS

Puddings and soufflés are a quick way to have a yummy desert without having to take the time to make a lengthy gourmet desert. For me, puddings and soufflés in individual servings are a comfort food, and take me back to childhood and happier times when life was simpler. Sometimes, just a couple of mouthfuls of a wonderful pudding are enough to make you happy or to curb that sweet dessert tooth.

Choco-Coco Pudding

Brenda Cobb, founder of Living Foods Institute and author of The Living Foods Lifestyle

Prep: 15 minutes
Soak: dates, 4–6 hours

2 cups dates, pitted and soaked
5 ripe avocados
1½ cups raw carob
1 cup Botanical Medica Raw Coconut Oil
½-1 cup date juice

Soak the dates 4–6 hours in filtered water, and then drain. Pit the dates and take off any hard stems. Scoop out the avocado from the shell, and then blend all the ingredients in a Vitamix®. Indulge!

Chia Pudding

Joel Odhner, Catalyst Cleanse, Rawlife Line, Philadelphia, PA

Prep: 15 minutes

1 cup chia seeds
4 cups So Delicious® coconut milk
⅓ cup maple syrup (or substitute stevia)
2 teaspoons vanilla
2 teaspoons cinnamon

Stir for 5 minutes until it thickens like pudding.

Strawberry-Mango Pudding

Potlucker Linda Cooper, Linda Louise Cakes

Prep: 20 minutes

7 mangoes, peeled and pitted
1 avocado
4 pounds strawberries (or to taste)

Blend all the ingredients together in a food processor until smooth and creamy.

Mango-Kiwi Soufflé

Sheryll Chavarria, Raw Can Roll Café and Pure Body Spa,
Douglassville, PA (www.rawcanrollcafe.com)

Prep: 15–20 minutes
Chill: 20 minutes in freezer (or 1 hour in refrigerator)

3 mangos, seeded and chopped
¼ cup agave
½ cup meat young Thai coconut
2 kiwis, peeled and sliced into rounds
Pinch sea salt

Blend mangos, salt, agave, and coconut meat together in a high-speed blender until creamy. Pour into a large bowl and stir in the kiwi, leaving some of the kiwi to garnish the top of the soufflé. Pour into individual bowls, and then place in the freezer for about 20 minutes (or in the refrigerator for about 1 hour) until it sets. Because this is so good, I typically end up eating it right away without waiting for it to chill, but you can serve it either way.

Coconut Rice Pudding with Peaches

Raw Chef Dan, Quintessence, New York, NY, and Crucina, Madrid, Spain

Prep: 20–30 minutes

3–4 young Thai coconuts (save the meat of 1 coconut and set aside)
1 cup really raw cashews
½ cup water
1 tablespoon vanilla flavoring
1 teaspoon sea salt
¼ cup raisins
Sliced peaches (to garnish)
Cinnamon (to garnish)

Chop and clean the coconuts, save the meat from 1 coconut, and put aside.

Place the remaining meat of the young coconuts in a food processor and pulse-chop until the coconut becomes a rice-like consistency. Pour into a mixing bowl and set aside. You will want about 1½-2 cups.

In a blender, combine the cashews, last coconut, water, vanilla, and salt until it forms a cream-like consistency.

Once smooth and creamy, pour the cream over your rice, mix well with the raisins, and refrigerate.

To serve, place 1 serving in a bowl, garnish with slices of ripe fresh peaches, and dust lightly with cinnamon.

Young Thai coconuts can be found in nearly any Asian market or Chinatown area of your nearest major city.

You can replace the coconut with yellow squash or even mix them together if you are short on coconut meat.

Chocolate Mousse

Raw Chef Dan, Quintessence, New York, NY, and Crucina,
Madrid, Spain

Prep: 15 minutes

1½ Haas avocados
⅔ cup coconut water
1 tablespoon alcohol-free vanilla extract
2 tablespoons cocoa
3 dates, pitted
1 teaspoon sea salt

Blend the above ingredients together until creamy. Serve in your favorite dish.

Avocado Vanilla Mousse

Raw Chef Dan, Quintessence, New York, NY, and Crucina,
Madrid, Spain

Prep: 15 minutes

2 large Hass avocados
6 dates, pitted
1 tablespoon alcohol-free vanilla extract
1 tablespoon sea salt
½ cup water

Place the above ingredients in a food processor with the S-blade, and blend until creamy. Add water for the desired consistency.

Chocolate Chia Pudding

*Raw Chef Dan, Quintessence, New York, NY, and Crucina,
Madrid, Spain*

Prep: 15 minutes

¼ cup chia seeds
1 cup chocolate cashew milk
½ teaspoon alcohol-free vanilla extract

Using a fork, mix all the ingredients and let sit for 2 hours, stirring
occasionally.

Coconut Chia Pudding

Raw Chef Dan, Quintessence, New York, NY, and Crucina, Madrid, Spain

1 young Thai coconut
2 tablespoons chia seeds

Cut open the coconut and pour the water from the coconut into a large glass. Place 6 ounces of the coconut water into a mixing bowl and add the chia seeds (you can drink any remaining coconut water). Mix the coconut water and chia seeds together, making sure that the seeds are thoroughly coated.

Let soak for about 20 minutes, stirring occasionally to prevent clumping. Then scrape all the meat loose inside the coconut, but leave it in the coconut. Pour the coco-chia concoction back into the coconut. Chill and serve cool.

> You can also add flavors such as vanilla, nutmeg, chai, or chopped banana and strawberry.